Pepper is a sled dog. She lives in Iqaluit, Nunavut with her family. Dad, Mom and two girls. She loooooves to play outside.

When the days are long, Pepper likes to watch the girls go berry picking.

She is an excellent watch dog.

She loves to watch the birds flying in the distance, the grass swaying in the breeze and ice floating in the river.

Good job Pepper!

Pepper loves to go clam digging and checking the nets for fish. Boating out is her favorite!

When there are fish to pull in, they wiggle and wriggle around at the bottom of the boat.

Sometimes they'll see seal in the bay too.

She thinks to herself: What is that sea puppy doing so far out in the water??? I love the water too, but not THAT much!

They'll turn the fresh fish from the nets into pipsi. The dried fish will last a lot longer. It's *really* good stuff!

Pepper would like a nibble but keeps her nose to herself.

Good job Pepper!

The girls are getting so grown up! Mom and Dad decide that they want the kids to go to a high school in Ottawa.

The family has been there lots of times so it’s not too hard to imagine living there.

So, the parents register the kids for school and they go in the fall.

Of course, Pepper is going too!

Good dog Pepper!

Pepper has family that live in Ottawa. She loves to spend time with them. Everyone loves to give her lots of pets because she’s the floofiest girl!

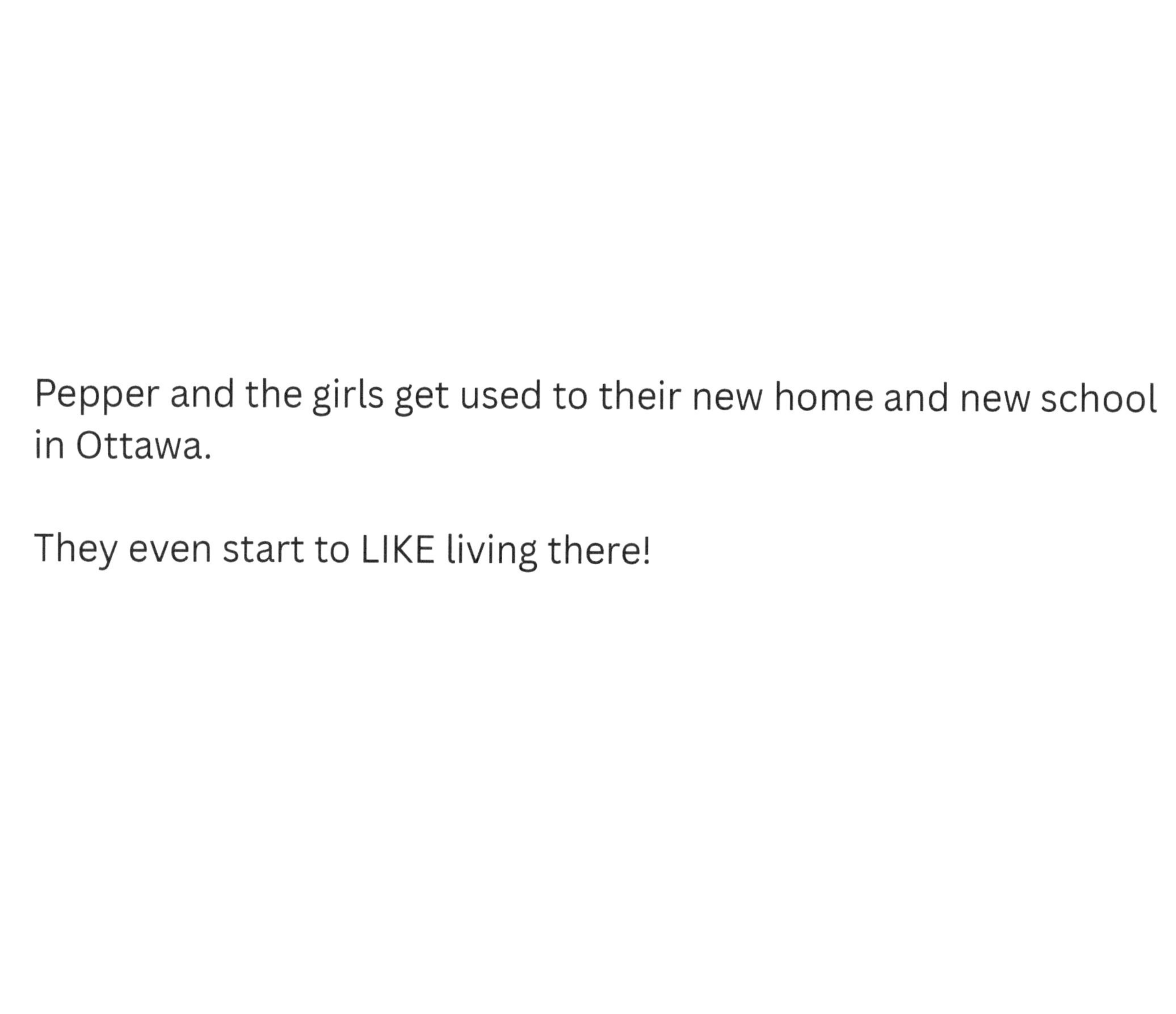
Pepper and the girls get used to their new home and new school in Ottawa.

They even start to LIKE living there!

The best part, is that they are together.

Good dog Pepper!

CHICKEN TENDERS

Pepper Moves to Ottawa

ISBN 979-8-234-01478-8

www.ingramcontent.com/pod-product-compliance
Ingram Content Group UK Ltd.
Pitfield, Milton Keynes, MK11 3LW, UK
UKHW060110300726
14090UKWH00002B/114

* 9 7 9 8 2 3 4 0 1 4 7 8 8 *